LET'S WRESTLE

D1458601

ALL MEN ARE BROTHERS AND WOMEN

Redstone Press
7a St Lawrence Terrace, London W10 5SU
www.redstonepress.co.uk

First Published 2004
Reprinted 2006

Artwork: Terence Smiyan,
and Otis Marchbank
Production: Tim Chester

ISBN-13 978-1-870003-09-4

ISBN-10 1-870003-09-8

A CIP record for this book is available from the British Library

GOD SAID "LET THERE BE LIGHT"
BUT THE LIGHT DIDN'T WORK
SO GOD TELEPHONED THE LANDLORD
BUT THE LANDLORD WASN'T IN
AND GOD SPOKE TO THE LANDLORD'S
SON
AND GOD TOLD THE LANDLORD'S
SON THAT THERE WAS NO LIGHT
AND THE LANDLORD'S SON SAID
THERE WAS NOTHING THAT
COULD BE DONE UNTIL THE
LANDLORD GOT BACK FROM
HOLIDAY

CHAPTER
ONE

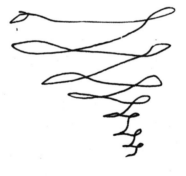

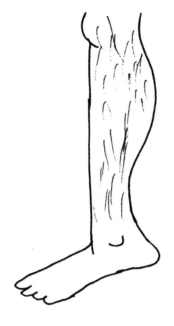

FROM THE KNEE DOWNWARDS
THAT IS ALL THAT YOU ARE
PERMITTED TO SEE. ANY MORE
THAN THAT ; THE THIGH , THE ARSE,
THE SCHLONG , THE ████ CONKERS,
THE TORSO , ETC ; I'M NOT
GOING TO SHOW YOU ANY OF
THAT AT THE MOMENT.

OLD BLACK BISCUIT

- WOULD YOU LIKE SOME ?
- YES PLEASE
- HERE YOU ARE
- THANK YOU (EATS)
    EERRRGGH ! THAT'S DISGUSTING!

THE ACTOR
DANIEL
DAY- LEWIS

MY BEER

I WANT MY BEER TO BE GOOD AND HONEST AND TRUE WITH A HINT OF THE UNKNOWN. I WANT MY BEER TO BE AUTHENTIC AND FRESH WITH AN EXPLOSIVE FINISH. I WANT MY BEER TO BE A FLAVOURSOME MASTERPIECE BREWED OUTSIDE THE UNITED KINGDOM BUT STILL WITHIN THE EUROPEAN ECONOMIC COMMUNITY. I WANT MY BEER TO BE STRONG AND HAVE INTEGRITY, LIKE MY FATHER AND TO BE KIND AND FORGIVING LIKE MY MOTHER. I DO NOT WANT MY BEER TO BE BITTER AND UNRELIABLE LIKE MY UNCLE PETE. AND I DON'T WANT IT TO TASTE OF METAL LIKE SOMEONE HAS PUT A POCKET FULL OF LOOSE CHANGE IN IT.

THE DAYTIME

I DRANK ALL THE BEER
I ATE ALL THE FOOD
I KILLED ALL THE BUGS
I ATE ALL THE BUGS

MY DEAR FREIND,

EVERYTHING I KNOW
ABOUT DECORATION AND
ADORNMENT I SHALL
BRING TO BEAR IN
ORDER THAT YOURWED-
DDING RECEPTION WILL
BE A TRUE SUCCESS!
I HAVE THE KNACK!

THE BUTTER

GLUEY

~~████~~ BRIGHT ORANGE
SMELLS LIKE VINEGAR
DROPPED FROM A PLANE
EATEN BY REFUGEES
AND ANIMALS

LUBRICATES MACHINERY
WARDS OFF DEATH
FOR THE TIME BEING

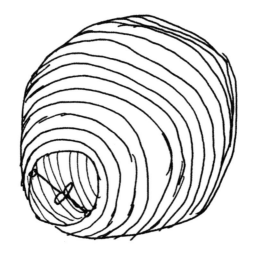

THE PAPER LANTERN

THE CRYSTAL BALL

THE CRYSTAL BALL FELL OFF ITS STAND ONTO THE FLOOR AND WAS DAMAGED. NOW IT DOES NOT SHOW THE FUTURE ACCURATELY. SOME OF THE THINGS IT SHOWS WILL COME TO PASS BUT SOME OF THE THINGS IT SHOWS WILL NOT COME TO PASS.

GRASS
CLIPPINGS

- ARE YOU MIROSLAV SLIVOVINOVICH?
- I AM
- THEN I BID YOU MIROSLAV SLIVOVINO-VICH COME WITH ME
- WHERE ARE WE GOING?
- WE ARE GOING DOWN THE SALT MINE
- WHY?
- ~~BECAS~~ BECAUSE YOU ARE NEEDED IN THE SALT MINE
- ~~BUT~~ BUT I KNOW NOTHING OF MINES OR OF SALT, WHAT USE COULD I BE THERE?
- THERE IS A GIFT FOR YOU DOWN THERE
- OH REALLY, WHAT IS IT?
- I THINK IT'S A NEW BICYCLE
- OH HOW SUPER! LET'S GO!
      (THEY GO DOWN THE SALT MINE)
- HERE IS YOUR GIFT MIROSLAV SLIVOVINOVICH
      (GIVES HIM SOME SALT)
- BUT YOU SAID I WAS GETTING A BICYCLE
- I THOUGHT YOU WERE BUT I WAS WRONG. ANYWAY WOULD YOU MIND MINING A BIT OF SALT WHILE YOU'RE DOWN HERE?
- OH ALL RIGHT THEN, PASS ME THE SPOON.

I FEEL SO SORRY FOR JIM
JIM LANGUISHES IN A PRISON CELL
WITH NO HOPE OF RELEASE
AND ALL JIM HAS TO READ
IS THIS BOOK WHICH IS ABOUT HOW
I FEEL SO SORRY FOR ~~____~~ HIM
AND HOW HE LANGUISHES IN A
PRISON CELL WITH NO HOPE
OF RELEASE

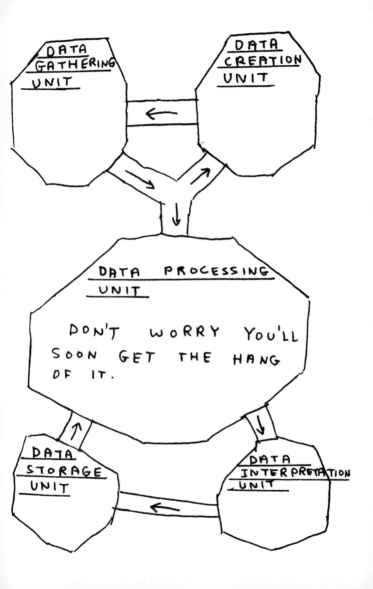

I STARED AT THIS APPLE FOR FIVE DAYS AND ROTTED IT WITH THE POWER OF MY MIND. OH HOW FRIGHT-ENING IT IS TO HAVE SUCH POWERFUL GIFTS. I BEG YOU TO TELL NO-ONE OR

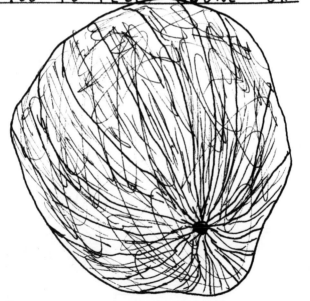

I SHALL BE BURNED AS A WITCH.

WORK

YOU GET A JOB AT THE
TODDLER FARM. BUT THE
TODDLERS TAKE AN INSTANT
DISLIKE TO YOU AND STAGE
A MUTINY. THEY SIT DOWN
AND REFUSE TO MOVE.
"PLEASE" YOU SAY

" PLEASE DON'T DO THIS. I
CAN'T AFFORD TO LOSE THIS
JOB BECAUSE I NEED THE
MONEY TO BUY CIGARS "

" WE DON'T CARE " SAY THE
TODDLERS " WE DON'T LIKE
YOU. WE THINK YOU'RE
PRETENTIOUS."

SO YOU LOSE YOUR JOB AND
YOU HAVE TO WORK IN AN
ABBATOIR WHERE THE CATTLE
DON'T LIKE YOU EITHER BUT IT DOESN'T
MATTER.

THE NAMES OF OUR COCKTAILS

LIVING WATERS
THE BEHAVIOUR OF BIRDS
GAS
SUPREME FANCY
MODERN THOUGHT
THE DRINK WITH NO NAME
RE-TRACE YOUR STEPS
AUTHORITY
THE BEATLES
HUMAN RIGHTS
I BEAR YOU NO MALICE
ALCOHOL'S BROTHER
A LESSER MIND
THE SEA
CAUSE AND EFFECT
TRANSGRESSION
ILLITERACY
DARLING BOOZE
SEPERATION FROM GOD

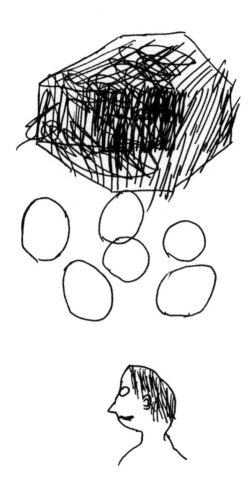

THIS IS THE MOST REVOLTING
THING I HAVE EVER SEEN
IT'S ABSOLUTELY DISGUSTING

I CAN SMELL MAGNETS
WHO'S GOT MAGNETS?
CAN YOU SMELL MAGNETS?
THERE IS AN UNMISTAKEABLE
SMELL OF MAGNETS AROUND
HERE. IT'S REALLY MAGNETY.

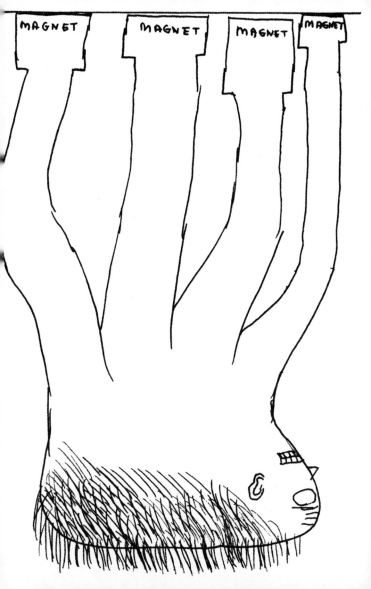

BEAR HOWLS YOUR NAME

WRITING IN A BAD LIGHT

I ATTEMPTS TO EULOGIZE BUT
AM THWARTED AGAIN BY
NOISE.

THEN I FORGETS WHAT IT WAS
THAT I WAS EULOGIZING
ABOUT.

IT OCCURS TO ME THEN
THAT I HAVE NOT GROWN AS
A WRITER ONE BIT AND
I DECIDES TO GIVE IT UP
HAVING ONLY WRITTEN ████
A HALF BOOK.

I RESOLVES TO WATCH TELLY.
ON THE TELLY IT IS 'THE
SEX LIVES OF SERPENTS' NARRATED
BY SOME OLD WIND BAG.
I AM HELD BY THE WAYS OF
THESE SNAKES AND THE QUEER
LOGIC OF THEIR DOINGS.
PLEASE KILL ME AND SPIT
ON MY GRAVE.

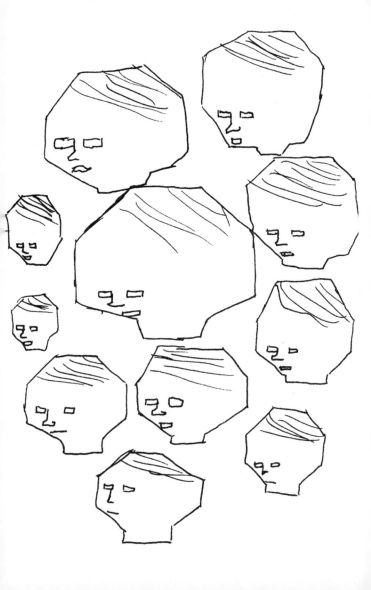

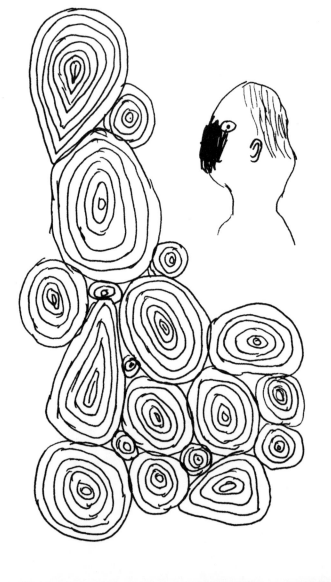

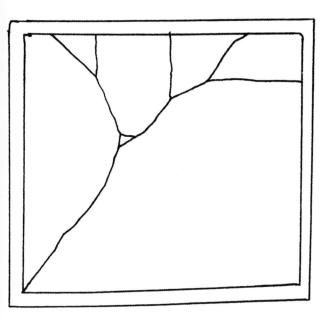

THE CRACKED WINDOW
OCCURED BY FREAKISH
ACCIDENT. I WAS TRYING
TO SWAT A FLY WITH ONE
OF MY SHOES.

NUTRITIONAL INFORMATION

ENERGY _ _ _ _ _ _ _ _ _ _ _ _ _ _ NONE
PROTEIN _ _ _ _ _ _ _ _ _ _ _ _ _ NONE
FAT _ _ _ _ _ _ _ _ _ _ _ _ _ _ _ NONE
CARBOHYDRATE _ _ _ _ _ _ _ _ NONE
SUGARS _ _ _ _ _ _ _ _ _ _ _ _ NONE
FIBRE _ _ _ _ _ _ _ _ _ _ _ _ _ NONE
SODIUM _ _ _ _ _ _ _ _ _ _ _ _ _ NONE

THE SILENCE TAKES SOME
GETTING USED TO BUT AFTER
A WHILE IT'S OK
YOU LISTEN TO YOUR HEART
BEATING AND YOU LISTEN
TO YOURSELF BREATHING
AND WHEN IT RAINS IT SOUNDS
DEAFENING

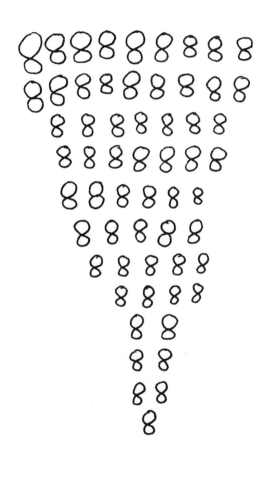

BEAR

(DANCING)

(AT REST)

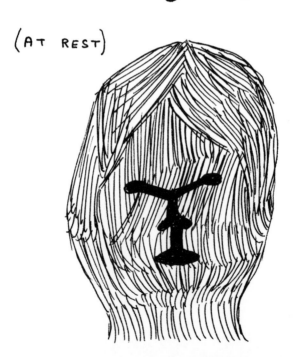

CONGRATULATIONS
ON MOVING IN
TO YOUR NEW
███ HOME

I AM SURE THAT ███ IT
WILL BE OK ███ ███
███ ███ ███ ███
███ ███ ███

ATTACK WHEN YOUR
ENEMY IS WEAK

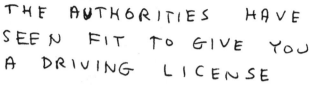

THE AUTHORITIES HAVE
SEEN FIT TO GIVE YOU
A DRIVING LICENSE

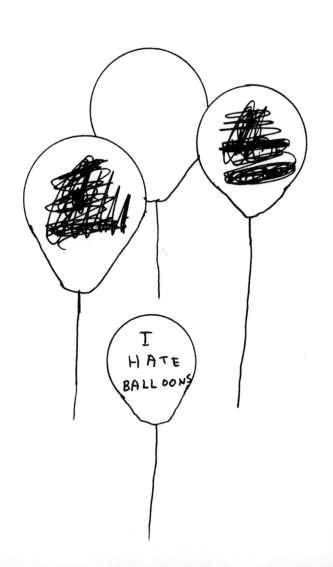

As I go up the steps
to receive my award
I wave to freinds and
family in the crowd

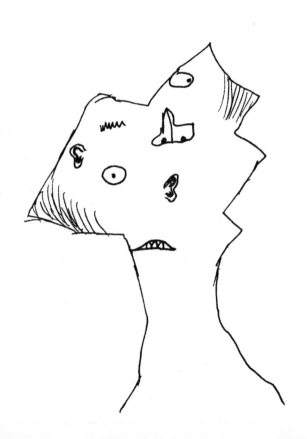

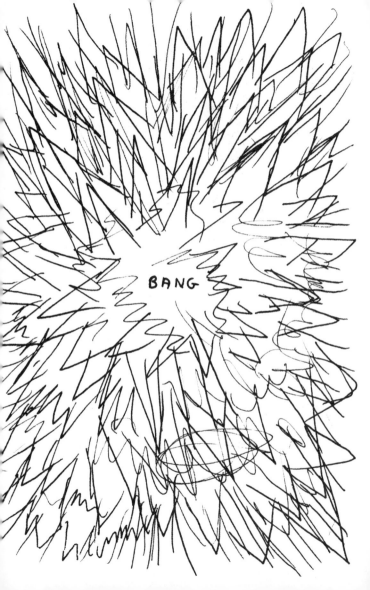

CAMPING —
NEVER AGAIN

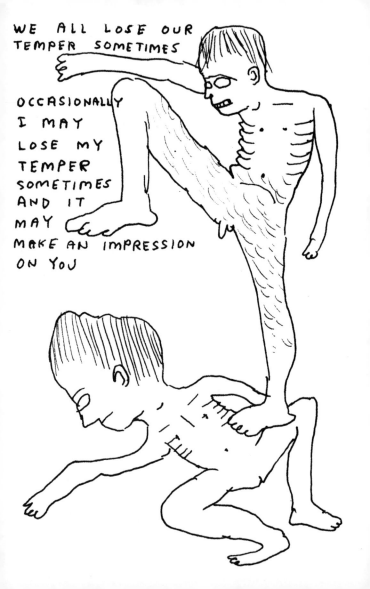

BEWARE OF THE SUBMERGED
ROCKS

WE MUST ALL OF US, YOU AND I AND EVERYONE, OCCUPY A SPACE.

AND THIS IS THE SPACE THAT I OCCUPY AT THE PRESENT TIME. IT IS ADEQUATE FOR MY NEEDS. IF AT SOME TIME IN THE FUTURE I FEEL THAT THIS SPACE NO LONGER MEETS MY REQUIRE-MENTS ; FOR INSTANCE IF I WISHED TO ACCOMODATE A GLASS TANK IN WHICH TO KEEP A LARGE REPTILE , THEN I WOULD PETITION FOR A LARGER SPACE . BUT UNTIL THAT TIME ARRIVES I AM JUST FINE RIGHT HERE, THANK — YOU VERY MUCH.

LEOPARD MAN

HIS BALLS

I HATE HIM

AND I AM ALLERGIC TO HIS KIND

BETWEEN ADVENTURES

BACK FROM THE MOUNTAINS

RETURNING HOM

RESTING

RESTING

RESTING

RETURN TO THE MOUNTAINS

I AM A VERY SHALLOW PERSON, I CANNOT
HELP IT, I WAS BORN SO.

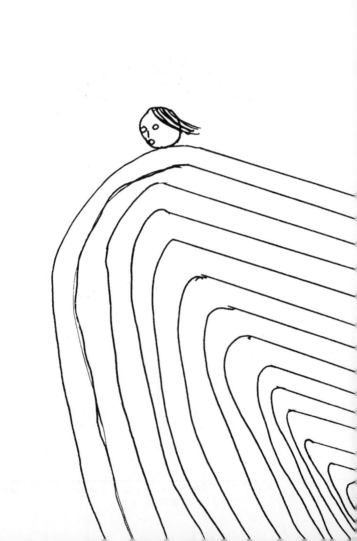

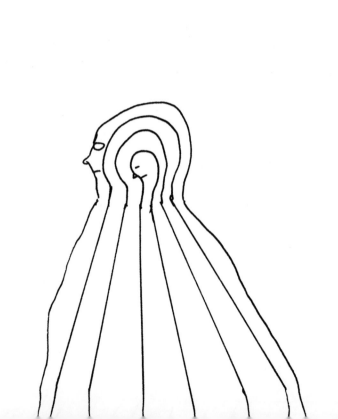

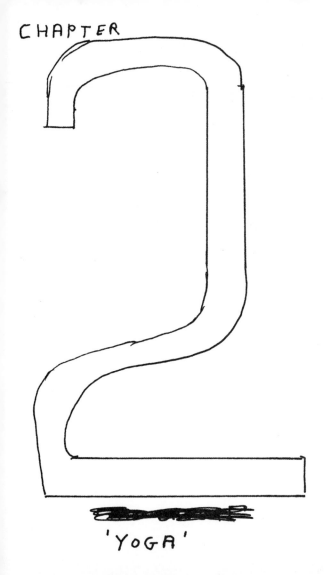

'YOGA'

STRANGE PHOBIAS

ONE MAN HAS A HORROR OF
BAKED BEANS

ANOTHER MAN IS SCARED OF
NEWSPAPER

THERE IS ALSO A WOMAN THAT
DOES NOT LIKE TREES AND
SHE THINKS SHE'S DROWNING
AND SHE ALSO FEELS TRAPPED

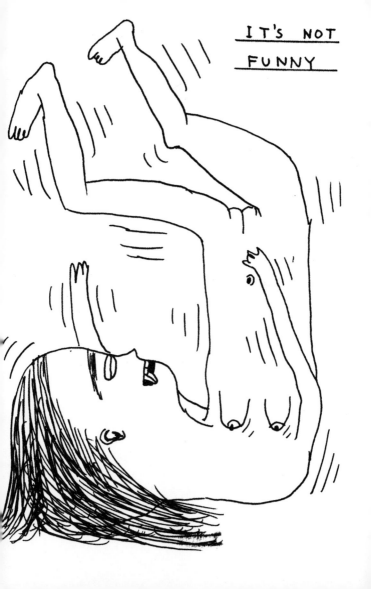

IT'S NOT
FUNNY

THE HUMAN CREATURE'S MERRIE
FORM : THE PHYSICIAN MUST
KNOW IT AND ALL ITS VAGUERY

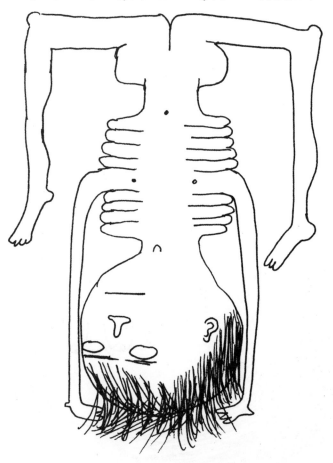

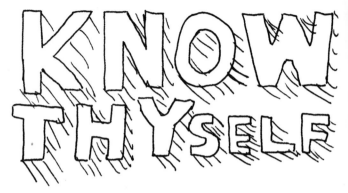

KNOW THYSELF

TEACH THYSELF THINGS

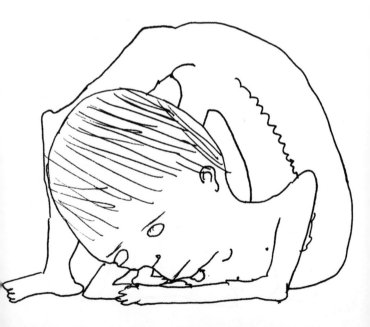

LIKE BIRDS

OUTSIDE ON THE ROOF

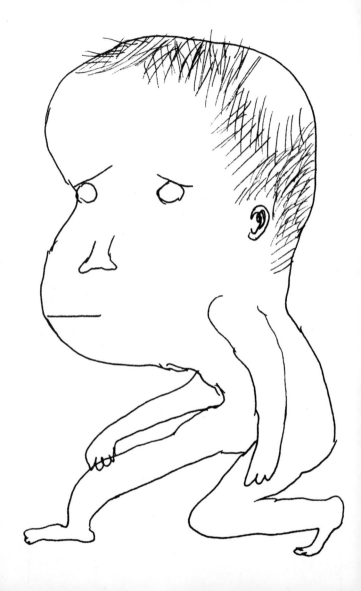

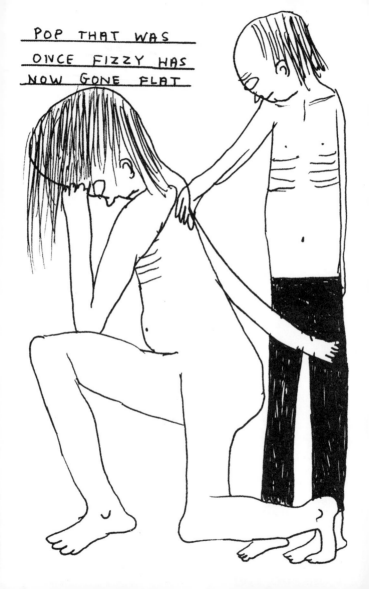

POP THAT WAS
ONCE FIZZY HAS
NOW GONE FLAT

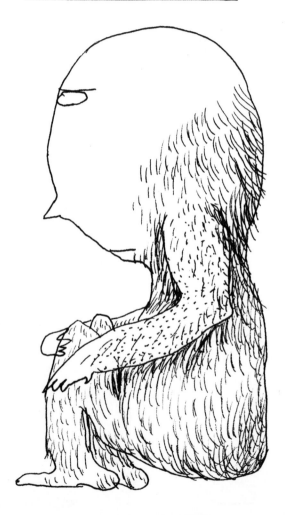

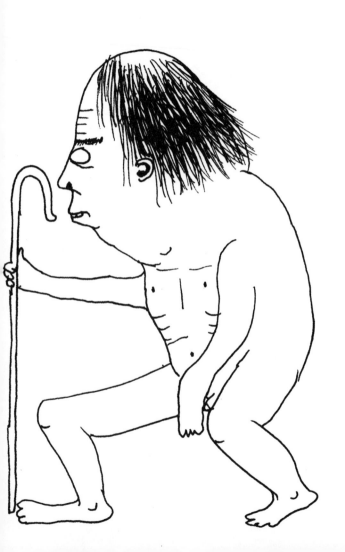

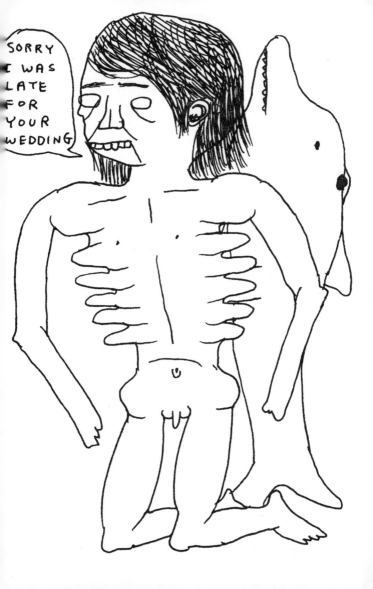

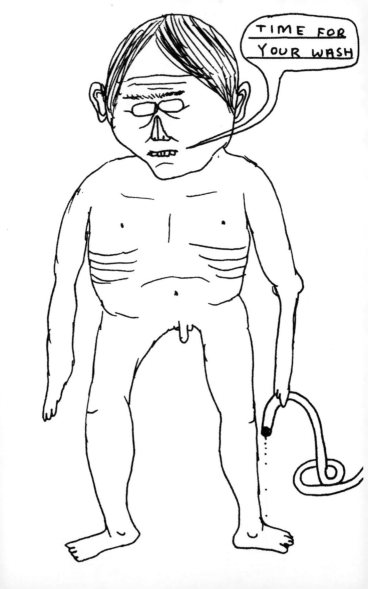

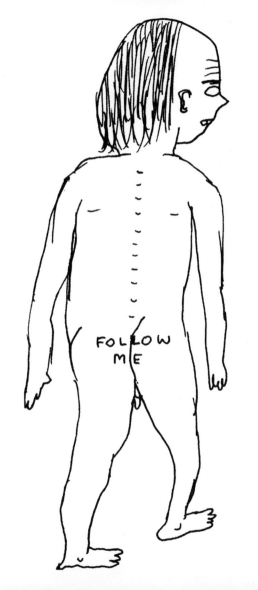

DON'T CALL ME SPUD

I DON'T LIKE IT

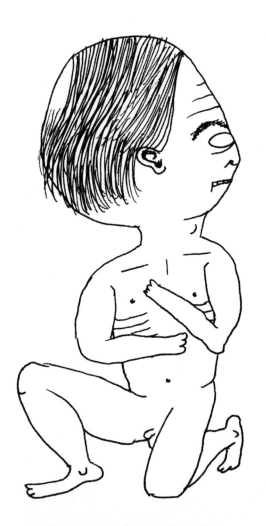

I WILL SHOUT YOUR NAME LOUDLY
FROM THE TOP OF MY VOICE
I WILL SCREECH IT OUT AT DAWN
LIKE A COCK CROWING
FOR ALL TO HEAR
AND IT WILL SOUND HORRIBLE
AND SARCASTIC
AND IT WILL TROUBLE YOU
AND I WILL DO IT EVERY DAY
FOR WEEKS
AND EACH TIME YOU HEAR IT YOU
WILL HAVE CAUSE TO STOP WHAT
YOU ARE DOING
AND LISTEN

MALCOLM

MAAALCOLM

MAAAAAAAALCOLM

MAAAAAAAAAAAAAAAA

AAAAAAALCOLM

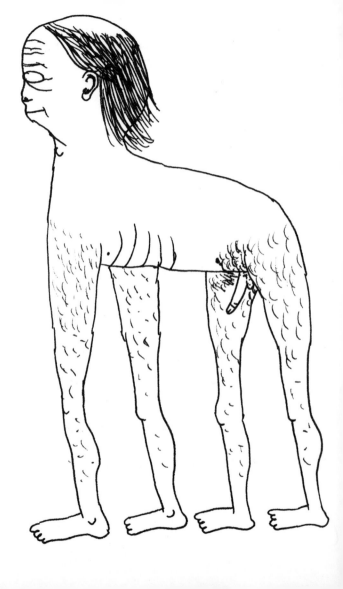

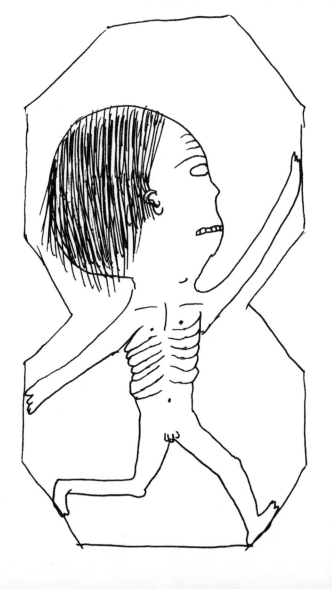

MARRY HER

SHE IS LIVELY AND
FULL OF FUN

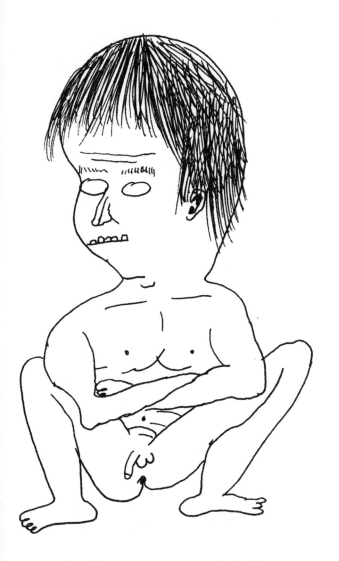

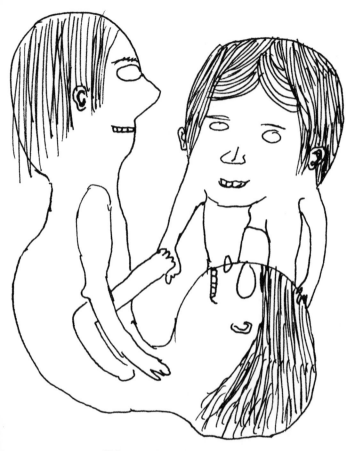

FREINDSHIP

BE CAREFUL WHO YOU MAKE FREINDS
WITH FOR ON ~~████~~ OCCASION FREINDS
CAN LEAD YOU ASTRAY AND MAKE YOU
DO THINGS THAT YOU DONT WANT TO DO.

MY FELLOW MAN

I WANT TO ASSIST HIM

I WANT TO HELP HIM

I WANT TO EARN HIS RESPECT

I WANT HIM TO LEARN FROM ME

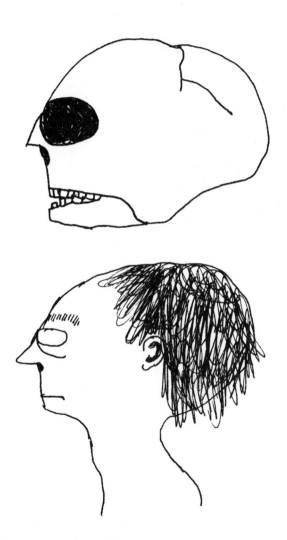

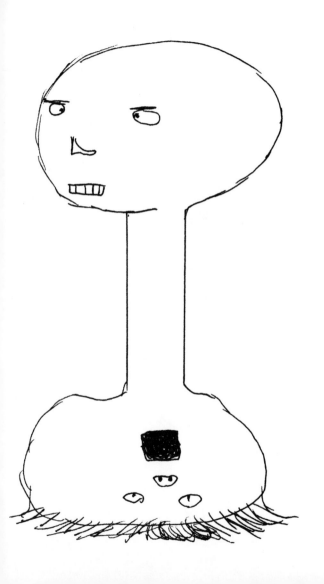

LET EACH BE ALLOWED
TO HAVE THEIR JOYS AND
INDULGEMENTS

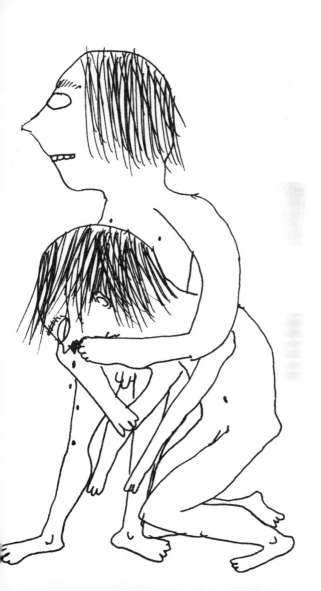

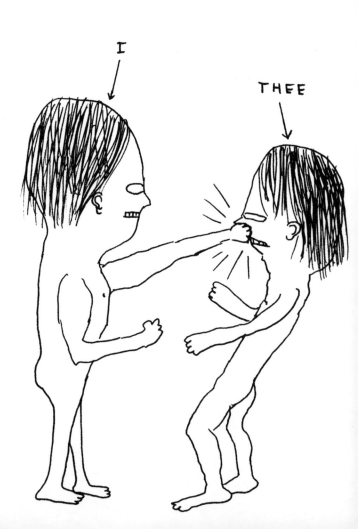

TRY NOT
TO LAUGH

CHILDREN : A NEW AND UNEXPECTED THREAT

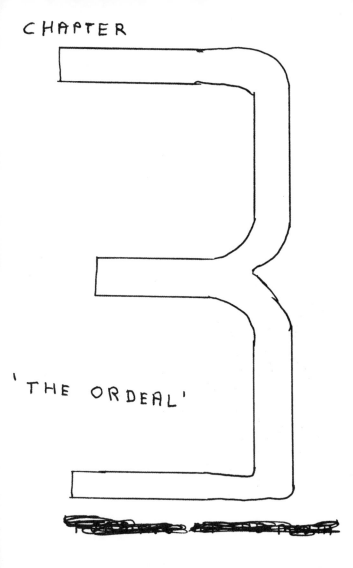

'THE ORDEAL'

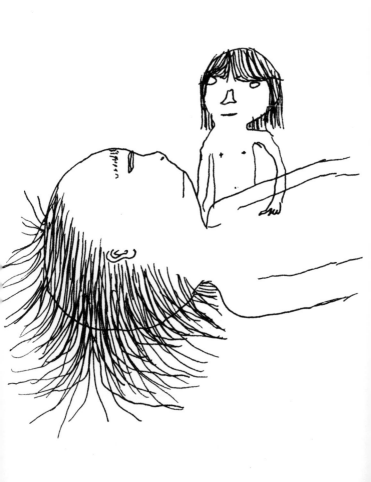

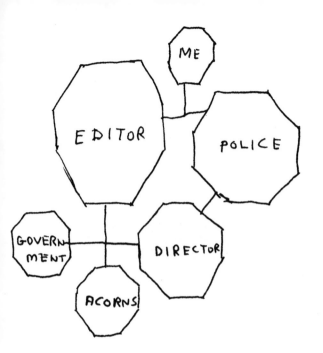

```
I WILL NOT LEAVE YOU ALONE
I WILL NOT LEAVE YOU ALONE
I WILL NOT LEAVE YOU ALONE
I WILL NOT LEAVE YOU ALONE
I WILL NOT LEAVE YOU ALONE
I WILL NOT LEAVE YOU ALONE
I WILL NOT LEAVE YOU ALONE
I WILL NOT LEAVE YOU ALONE
I WILL NOT LEAVE YOU ALONE
I WILL NOT LEAVE YOU ALONE
I WILL NOT LEAVE YOU
I WILL NOT LEAVE
I WILL NOT LEAVE
I WILL NOT LEAVE
I WILL NOT
I WILL NOT
I WILL NOT
I WILL NOT
I WILL NOT
I WILL NOT
I WILL NOT
I WILL NOT
I WILL NOT
I WILL NOT
I WILL NOT
I WILL NOT
I WILL NOT
```

MAN ON THE BUS TOLD ME
ABOUT A DREAM HE HAD
WHERE AN OCTOPUS SPUN
A GIANT WEB LIKE A
SPIDER

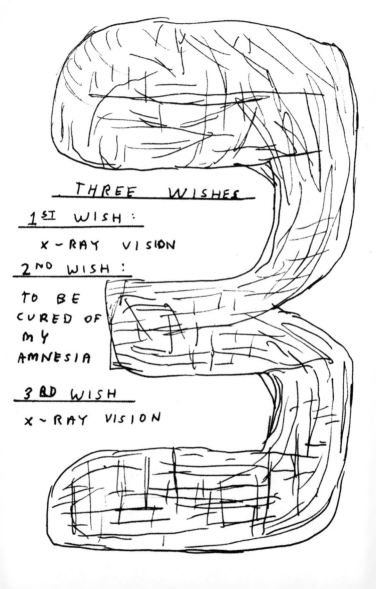

THREE WISHES

1ST WISH:

X - RAY VISION

2ND WISH:

TO BE
CURED OF
MY
AMNESIA

3RD WISH

X - RAY VISION

HE NEVER WANTED TO BE
THE CENTRE OF ATTENTION
HE WANTED TO BE INVISIBLE
BUT THEN HE HAD AN
EPILEPTIC FIT
AND HE BECAME THE CENTRE
OF ATTENTION

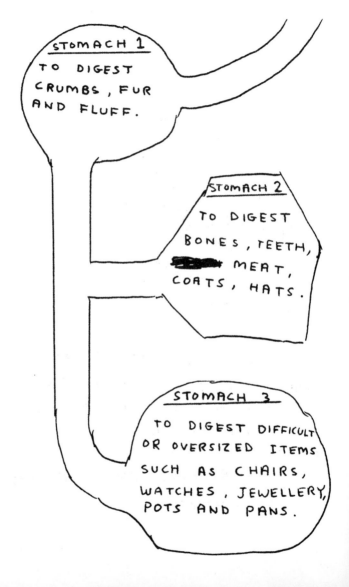

LATELY

I STOPPED WATCHING TELEVISION
AND READING THE NEWSPAPER
BUT IT MADE NO DIFFERENCE
I STOPPED WEARING SPECTACLES
BUT IT MADE NO DIFFERENCE
I STOPPED SAYING MY PRAYERS
BUT IT MADE NO DIFFERENCE
I STOPPED ANSWERING THE TELEPHONE
AND I STOPPED TYING MY SHOELACES
AND BRUSHING MY HAIR
AND I STOPPED WEARING CLOTHES
AND I STOPPED FEEDING THE DOG
AND HE RAN AWAY AND I DIDN'T CARE
AND I STOPPED TURNING THE LIGHT
ON AT NIGHT
AND I STOPPED OPENING THE
CURTAINS DURING THE DAY
AND I STOPPED GOING TO WORK
AND I STOPPED SPEAKING
AND I STOPPED GOING OUTSIDE
BUT IT DIDN'T MAKE ANY DIFFERENCE
NOBODY NOTICED NOT EVEN THE POSTMAN
AND THE DOG CAME BACK
AND I STARTED FEEDING HIM AGAIN
AND I THINK IT MADE US BOTH
FEEL BETTER

ENQUIRY

Q - DO YOU HAVE A NEEDLE?

A - I HAVE A SCREW

Q - A SCREW IS NO GOOD. IT IS NOT SHARP ENOUGH. DO YOU HAVE A NEEDLE?

A - I HAVE PEN

Q - A PEN IS NO GOOD. I WANT A NEEDLE

A - I HAVE A SPOON

Q - BUT I MUST HAVE A NEEDLE

A - I HAVE A WOK

Q - WHAT'S A WOK

A - IT'S A KIND OF FRYING PAN

Q - IS IT SHARP?

A - NO, IT IS ROUNDED

Q - THEN IT IS NO GOOD TO ME. DO YOU HAVE NEEDLE?

A - YES

Q - CAN I HAVE IT?

A - NO

ALLERGIC TO UPHOLSTERY

INITIALLY:

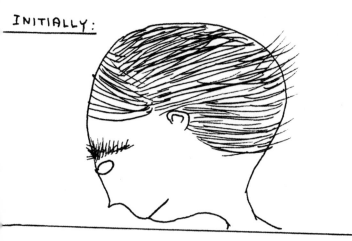

AFTER 10 MINUTES:

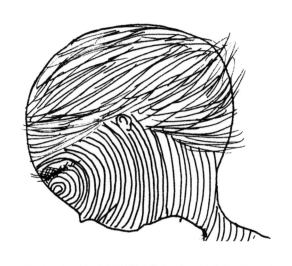

SNOW FALLS
SNOWMAN IS BUILT BY CHILDREN
SNOWMAN IS DISMANTLED BY
OTHER CHILDREN
SNOW MELTS

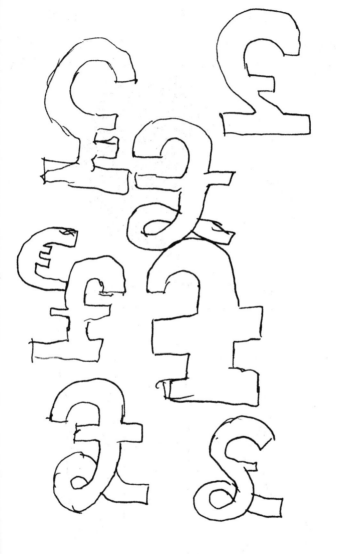

I CAN LIFT YOU UP
AND THROW YOU AROUND
AS IF YOU WERE A BAG

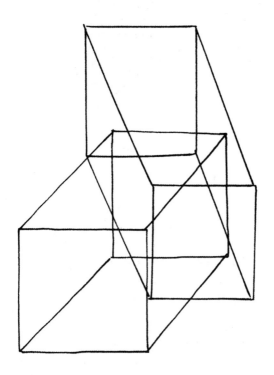

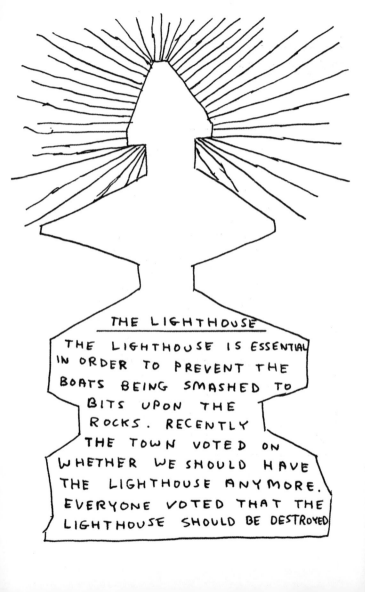

THE LIGHTHOUSE

THE LIGHTHOUSE IS ESSENTIAL IN ORDER TO PREVENT THE BOATS BEING SMASHED TO BITS UPON THE ROCKS. RECENTLY THE TOWN VOTED ON WHETHER WE SHOULD HAVE THE LIGHTHOUSE ANYMORE. EVERYONE VOTED THAT THE LIGHTHOUSE SHOULD BE DESTROYED

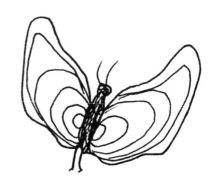

DAMN IT

ALL YOU
HAVE TO DO
IS CARRY
OUT THE
PROCEEDURES
AS THEY
ARE
DESCRIBED

DO NOT ENTER MY
PERSONAL SPACE
YOU ARE NOT WELCOME
SINCE ~~■~~ YOUR PRESENCE
INTERFERES WITH MY
LIFESTYLE
AND GIVES ME A HEADACHE

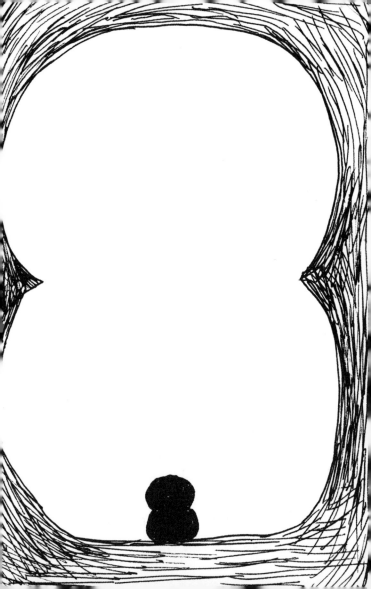

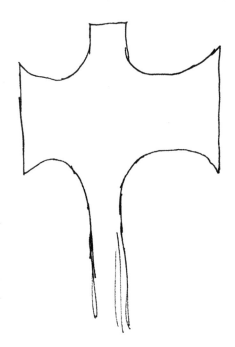

- WHAT IS YOUR FAVOURITE
CREATURE ?
- MY FAVOURITE CREATURE IS
THE AXE
- THE AXE IS NOT A CREATURE
IT IS A TOOL
- IS THE RAVEN A CREATURE ?
- YES
- THEN THE RAVEN IS MY FAVOURITE

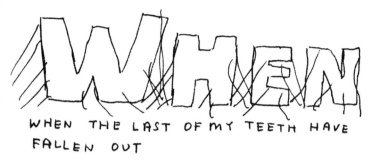

WHEN

WHEN THE LAST OF MY TEETH HAVE
FALLEN OUT

I WILL TAKE OFF ALL OF MY
CLOTHES AND

I WILL LIE ON THE GROUND
AND PRETEND TO BE DEAD

A TERRIBLE THOUGHT

THE
THOUGHT'S
DARK CENTRE

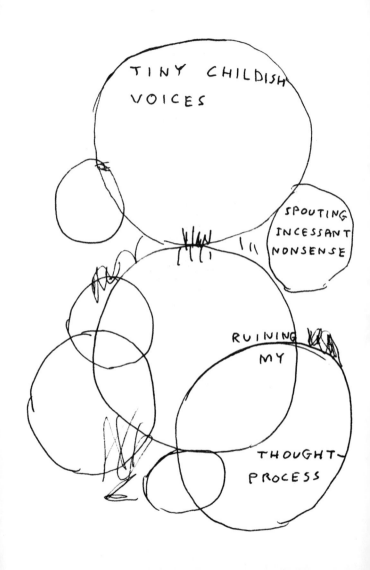

I'VE COME TO UN-BLOCK YOUR TOILET

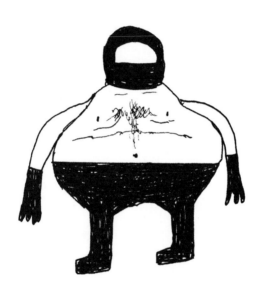

WHEN I'VE FINISHED I'M GOING TO GO TO SLEEP IN YOUR BED

HARSH WORLD OF SHAPES:
WEAK CUBE WILL BE KILLED

HEXAGONS WILL ATTACK AND
KILL DEFORMED SHAPE

THE PAIN IN MY HAND

THE PAIN IN MY
HAND IS EXCRUCIATIN

THE ULTIMATE DESTINY OF THE FRUIT

THE ULTIMATE DESTINY OF THE FRUIT IS EITHER TO BE EATEN OR TO GO MOULDY. IT'S A TERRIBLE CHOICE FOR THE FRUIT TO HAVE TO MAKE.

I AM VISITED BY A BEAST

WHEN ARE YOU GOING TO

ADMIT

THAT YOU

LOVE ME?

SAYS THE BEAST.
AND I SAY:

WHEN ALL OTHER POSSIBILITIES
HAVE BEEN EXHUASTED AND
WHEN I AM CERTAIN THAT
THERE CANNOT BE ANYTHING
BETTER AND WHEN I HAVE
TRIED ABSOLUTELY EVERYTHING
AND I AM AT MY FINAL,
LOWEST EBB.

A WOL IS SITTING ON
A BRANCH. THE WOL ~~MOUSE~~
SPYS A MOUSE. THE WOL
SWOOPS DOWN AND EATS
THE MOUSE.
THE WOL GOES BACK TO
THE BARN WHERE IT LIVES
AND SHITS OUT THE MOUSE
SKELETON ON THE BARN
FLOOR. A MAN COMES AND
SIFTS THOUGH THE WOL SHIT
TO FIND THE SKELETONS OF
ALL THE MICE THE WOL
HAS EATEN. THE MAN
MAKES A SCULPTURE.
HUNDREDS OF TINY MOUSE
SKULLS MAKING A SPHERE.

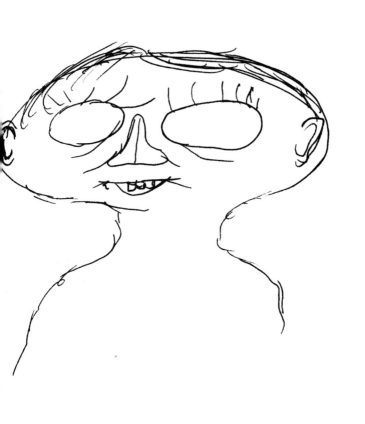

NOTES